COOL CARS

PORSCHE TAYCAN

BY THOMAS K. ADAMSON

BELLWETHER MEDIA ››› MINNEAPOLIS, MN

**EPIC BOOKS** are no ordinary books. They burst with intense action, high-speed heroics, and shadows of the unknown. Are you ready for an Epic adventure?

This edition first published in 2023 by Bellwether Media, Inc.

No part of this publication may be reproduced in whole or in part without written permission of the publisher. For information regarding permission, write to Bellwether Media, Inc., Attention: Permissions Department, 6012 Blue Circle Drive, Minnetonka, MN 55343.

Library of Congress Cataloging-in-Publication Data

LC record for Porsche Taycan available at: https://lccn.loc.gov/2022020246

Text copyright © 2023 by Bellwether Media, Inc. EPIC and associated logos are trademarks and/or registered trademarks of Bellwether Media, Inc.

Editor: Kieran Downs    Series Designer: Jeffrey Kollock    Book Designer: Josh Brink

Printed in the United States of America, North Mankato, MN

# TABLE OF CONTENTS

| ELECTRIC SPEED | 4 |
| ALL ABOUT THE TAYCAN | 6 |
| PARTS OF THE TAYCAN | 12 |
| THE TAYCAN'S FUTURE | 20 |
| GLOSSARY | 22 |
| TO LEARN MORE | 23 |
| INDEX | 24 |

# ELECTRIC SPEED »

The driver pushes the brake pedal of their Porsche Taycan. Then they press the **accelerator**. The dashboard reads "launch control activated."

The driver releases the brake. The **electric car** speeds forward. It zips away quietly!

### TAYCAN'S NAME

Taycan is a blend of two Turkish words. The name means "soul of a spirited young horse."

# ALL ABOUT THE TAYCAN ≫

**1948 PORSCHE 356**

Porsche's first sports car was built in 1948. Porsches are known for their comfort. They are also fast!

> Porsche's most famous **model** is the 911. Other well-known models include the Cayman and the 918 Spyder.

**2022 PORSCHE 911 GTS**

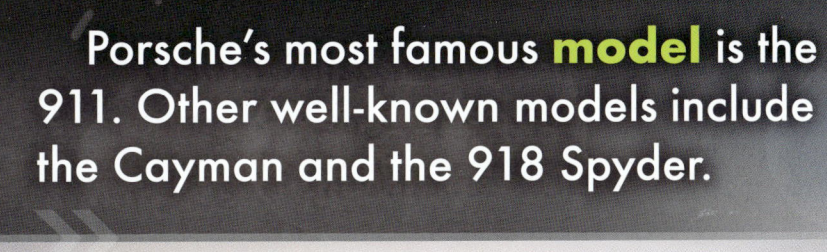

## 📍 WHERE IS IT MADE?

**EUROPE**

**ZUFFENHAUSEN, GERMANY**

7

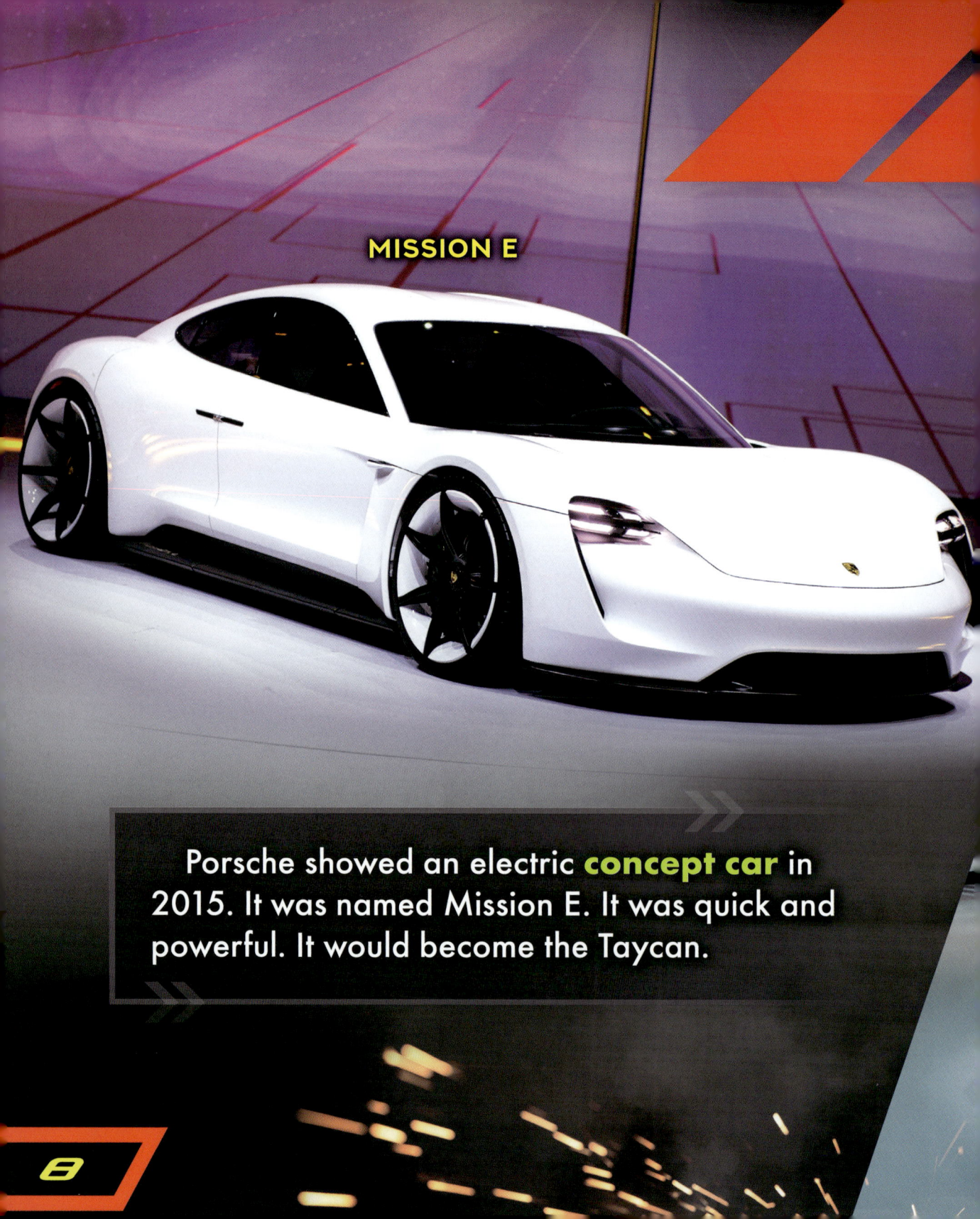

## MISSION E

Porsche showed an electric **concept car** in 2015. It was named Mission E. It was quick and powerful. It would become the Taycan.

The Taycan was the first all-electric car sold by Porsche. It went on sale in 2019.

**ROOM IN THE BACKSEAT**
All Taycans are 4-door models.

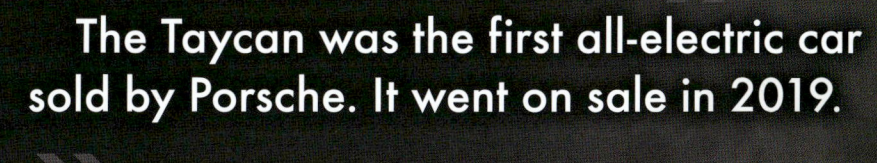

The Taycan has a heated steering wheel. It also has heated seats. **Touch screens** show the current **battery** charge. They also control the vents and headlights.

STEERING WHEEL

#  TAYCAN BASICS

| YEAR FIRST MADE | 2019 |
| --- | --- |
| COST | starts at $86,700 |
| HOW MANY MADE | 38,474 in 2021 |

### FEATURES

electric motor

charging ports

touch screens

TOUCH SCREEN

# PARTS OF THE TAYCAN >>

The Taycan's electric **motor** is powered by batteries. The heavy batteries are under the floor.

This gives the car a low **center of gravity**. It can take corners quickly.

## MOTOR SPECS

**ELECTRIC MOTOR** >>

**TOP SPEED** — up to 162 miles (261 kilometers) per hour

**0-60 TIME** — 2.6 seconds or less

**HORSEPOWER** — up to 750 hp

**PARKING**

Drivers can park their Taycan with their smartphones!

The Taycan has **charging ports** on both sides. Its batteries can recharge in about 20 minutes at a **charging station**.

## SIZE CHART

**WIDTH** 77.5 inches (196.9 centimeters)

The Taycan has a long **range**. Some models can travel 280 miles (451 kilometers) before needing a recharge.

TAYCAN TURBO S

**HEIGHT** 54.9 inches (139.4 centimeters)

**LENGTH** 195.4 inches (496.3 centimeters)

The Turbo S is the most powerful Taycan model. Its motor sends extra power to the wheels.

## TAYCAN CROSS TURISMO

The Cross Turismo is an off-road model. It has higher **clearance** for bumpy roads.

The Taycan is speedy. The most powerful model has a 750-**horsepower** motor. It reaches 60 miles (97 kilometers) per hour in 2.6 seconds.

Its top speed is 162 miles (261 kilometers) per hour!

# THE TAYCAN'S FUTURE »

The Taycan is one of Porsche's top-selling cars. The company is making new Taycan models. The Taycan GTS and GTS Sport Turismo look sportier.
These electric cars are the future of Porsche!

**TAYCAN GTS SPORT TURISMO**

PORSCHE TAYCAN BEING BUILT

# GLOSSARY

**accelerator**—the foot pedal in a car that makes the car move

**battery**—a part that supplies electric energy to a car

**center of gravity**—the point where an object's weight is even on all sides

**charging ports**—openings that allow a charger to connect to an electric vehicle

**charging station**—a place where electric cars are plugged in to charge

**clearance**—the space between the bottom of a car and the ground; clearance is needed for a car to move freely without bumping anything on the road or the ground.

**concept car**—a car built to show a new design

**electric car**—a car powered completely by electricity

**horsepower**—a measurement of the power of an engine or motor

**model**—a specific kind of car

**motor**—a machine that gives something the power to move

**range**—the distance a car can travel without refueling or recharging

**touch screens**—displays on which people can select options by touching the screens

# TO LEARN MORE

### AT THE LIBRARY

Colby, Jennifer. *Porsche*. Ann Arbor, Mich.: Cherry Lake Publishing, 2022.

Garstecki, Julia. *Porsche 911 GT3*. Mankato, Minn.: Black Rabbit Books, 2020.

Sommer, Nathan. *Lotus Evija*. Minneapolis, Minn.: Bellwether Media, 2023.

### ON THE WEB

Factsurfer.com gives you a safe, fun way to find more information.

1. Go to www.factsurfer.com.

2. Enter "Porsche Taycan" into the search box and click 🔍.

3. Select your book cover to see a list of related content.

# INDEX

accelerator, 4
basics, 11
battery, 10, 12, 14
brake pedal, 4, 5
charging ports, 14
charging station, 14
clearance, 17
company, 6, 7, 8, 9, 20
Cross Turismo, 17
electric car, 5, 8, 9, 20
GTS, 20
GTS Sport Turismo, 20
history, 6, 8, 9
Mission E, 8
models, 7, 8, 9, 15, 16, 17, 18, 20
motor, 12, 16, 18

motor specs, 12
name, 5
range, 15
seats, 10
size chart, 14–15
smartphones, 13
speed, 5, 6, 8, 18, 19
steering wheel, 10
touch screens, 10, 11
Turbo S, 15, 16
Zuffenhausen, Germany, 7

The images in this book are reproduced through the courtesy of: Julia Lav, front cover (car); ESB Professional, front cover (background); ZOOMeep, p. 3; supergenijalac, pp. 4, 5; Dmitry Orlov/ Alamy, p. 6; Gabriel Nica, p. 7; ODD ANDERSEN/ Getty Images, p. 8; Bloomberg/ Getty Images, pp. 9, 20, 21; Sjoerd van der Wal/ Getty Images, pp. 10-11 (interior); VanderWolf Images, p. 11 (Taycan); dpa/ Alamy, p. 11 (electric motor); Wing Lun Leung, p. 11 (charging ports); AJM681/ Alamy, p. 11 (touch screen); Roman Stasiuk/ Alamy, p. 12; picture alliance/ Getty Images, p. 12 (electric motor); Pontus Lundahl/ TT/ Alamy, p. 13; Grzegorz Czapski/ Alamy, p. 14; Dmitry Orlov, p. 14 (size chart); Halil Dorukhan Mercan/ Alamy, p. 15; Dary423, p. 15 (size chart); Mariusz Burcz/ Alamy, p. 16 (Taycan Turbo S); BoJack, p. 17 (Taycan Cross Turismo); ZUMA Press, Inc./ Alamy, p. 18; y_carfan, p. 19.